GRADUATION

INSPIRATION

1

AVONSIDE
PRESS

Graduation Inspiration

1

*Inspiring Quotes from the World's
Most Uplifting Graduation Speeches:*

*How to Escape the Hamster Wheel
and Live the Life You Want*

Edited by
Alison Wilson

First published in 2015 by Avonside Press

ISBN: 978-0-9942855-0-8

Avonside Press Pty Ltd
PO Box 174, Freshwater Beach, NSW 2096
Australia

Since you cannot experience everything, you need the experiences of others - especially the Beluga Caviar, the quotations!

They are the most precious eggs of the big life experiences.

Mehmet Murat ildan

Other Books by Alison Wilson

Graduation Inspiration 2

Graduation Inspiration 3

Hold The Phone:
The Definitive Guide to How to Protect Your Health from Phones and Wireless

Hold The Phone: Here's Why:
Advice from the Experts on How Phones and Wireless Affect Health

Websites:

www.holdthephone.co

www.graduationinspiration.com

Contents

Intro

Maybe you're at the beginning of your adult life and looking toward the future, wondering how it's going to go, and perhaps considering what you 'should' be doing.

Or you may be further down the track and circumstances mean that you're being 'encouraged' by Life to have a rethink about the way you're heading.

Either way, the aim of this book is to give you some hope and inspiration, and alternative views on the inside track from others who've gone before . . .

Others who've looked life in the eye, gone a few rounds and often been beaten up a little. Others who have come out the other end with time-saving tips for you on what they've found are the priorities in life.

Most importantly, they offer insight into how to live a life that is much more likely to bring you success.

The definition of 'success' here includes happiness, fulfilment, good relationships – and a sense of calm, contentment and true meaning. A life less ordinary in fact.

The speakers here are not only included because of their accomplishments, they're here because they have something insightful and inspiring – and optimistic – to say.

The most important thing about their speeches was their generosity. They didn't focus on themselves – but on you. They spent their time attempting to pass on something helpful and valuable – in all probability not even realising how far their inspiration would reach.

Reading their words will allow you to look at where your life is going, and how it's going. It's a chance to see if there's any room to make it flow a little easier, and become a whole lot more interesting and rewarding.

"You are capable of more than you think."

Bradley Whitford

What They've Got To Say:

The Quotes

OVERCOMING FEAR

Having fear, and then proceeding in spite of it, is where REAL confidence comes from.

It's the accumulation of experiences in your life in which you overcome your fear and try something, even if you really do fail at it!

That leads to authentic self-esteem.

Savannah Guthrie
Hobart & William Smith Colleges 2012

Lean into risk.

Believe me, 95 per cent of the people who take risks - whether it works out or not - are glad they did it.

David Brooks
Sewanee University of The South 2013

Overcoming Fear

You don't have to be fearless - just don't let fear stop you. Live like this as best as you can, and I guarantee you will look back at a life well lived.

Stay young at heart. Stay hungry. Take those risks.

Charlie Day
Merrimack College 2014

You never know what is around the corner unless you peek. Hold someone's hand while you do it. You will feel less scared . . .

Besides, it is much more fun to succeed and fail with other people.

Amy Poehler
Harvard 2011

What I wish someone would've told me before I stepped out in the world. And the first thing is: Stop worrying so much, OK?

Stop being scared of the unknown, because anything I worried about didn't happen.

Other stuff happened, but not what I worried about.

Sandra Bullock
Warren Easton Charter School 2014

Ask yourself one question:
If I didn't have to do it perfectly, what would I try?

Jerry Zucker
University of Wisconsin-Madison 2013

Overcoming Fear

I'm telling you right now, courage does not always roar.

It's not when you stand up and beat your chest and you're ready for the big game, the big fight, the big speech. That is not real courage in my book anymore. It's not running into a burning building.

Real courage is that when life has beaten you down so low, when you are broken, when you have wounds that you wonder if they could ever heal . . .

Courage is when you've done something wrong and you feel the weight of shame on your chest, so heavy that you can barely breathe.

Courage is when you're curled up in a ball on your bed sleepless throughout the night and when the sun comes up, courage isn't the roar, courage is that small voice in your mind that says:

"Get up, get out of bed, put your feet on the floor, brush your teeth, wash your face, comb your hair – God, if you have it – put your hand on that door knob and go outside for another day of loving, and stand with all of your might and look up into the heavens."

And courage has you say in a defiant spirit:

"You can take everything from me, you could cut me deep, you could render me in shame, but you will never, ever, stop me from loving."

Cory Booker
Stanford 2012

Overcoming Fear

Don't be afraid to fail. There are plenty of second, third and countless chances to change . . .

M L Flynn
Hollins College 1995

If you strike the right relationship with your fear, it can tell you a lot of really exciting things besides simply just what to be afraid of . . .

That tension will always be there, but so long as your desire to explore is greater than your desire to not screw up, you're on the right track.

A life oriented toward discovery is infinitely more rewarding than a life oriented toward not blowing it.

Ed Helms
Knox College 2013

Be fearless.

Have the courage to take risks.
Go where there are no guarantees.

Get out of your comfort zone - even if it means being uncomfortable.

Katie Couric
Williams College 2007

You cannot succeed without this risk of failure. You cannot have a voice without the risk of criticism.

And you cannot love without the risk of loss.

You must take these risks.

Charlie Day
Merrimack College 2014

OVERCOMING FEAR

Don't let your fears overwhelm your desire.

Let the barriers you face – and there will be barriers - be external, not internal.

Fortune does favor the bold, and I promise that you will never know what you're capable of unless you try.

Sheryl Sandberg
Barnard College 2011

Have courage still – and persevere. All work that is worth anything is done in faith.

Madeleine Albright
Mount Holyoke College 1997

Overcoming Fear

Don't be afraid of fear . . .

Indeed, the truth about fear, as with the rest of life, is that you'll only really figure it out by living through it.

So, by God, get out there and live.

Take your lumps. Dole out a few lumps.
And trust you'll figure it out.

Trust your instincts.
Trust your passions.
Trust your empathy.

And trust your love.

Ed Helms
Knox College 2013

13

Overcoming Fear

I've come to learn in my life to embrace discomfort because it's a precondition to service.

I've come to realize to embrace fear because, if you can move through fear, you find out that fear is a precondition to discovery.

I've learned in my life to embrace frustration because, when you get really frustrated, that is a precondition to incredible breakthroughs.

Cory Booker
Stanford 2012

Reframing 'Success' and 'Failure'

I've interviewed hundreds of extremely successful people, and among those who are rich and famous, the vast majority made money and became prominent not because they pursued riches and fame, but only as a side effect of doing what they love.

In fact, the Harvard psychologist Daniel Gilbert has spent decades studying happiness and he found that cash and contentment are almost completely disconnected.

Katie Couric
Williams College 2007

If you don't fail, you're not even trying.

Denzel Washington
University of Pennsylvania 2011

16

Don't spend a lot of time worrying about your failures.

I've learned a whole lot more from my mistakes than from all of my successes.

Ann Richards
Mount Holyoke College 1995

Failure is not the opposite of success; it's an integral part of success.

And that means not letting the fears in our heads get in our way.   Not letting that voice of doubt have the last word.

Arianna Huffington
Sarah Lawrence College 2011

Failure gave me an inner security that I had never attained by passing examinations.

Failure taught me things about myself that I could have learned no other way.

The knowledge that you have emerged wiser and stronger from setbacks means that you are, ever after, secure in your ability to survive.

J K Rowling
Harvard 2008

Recognize that there will be failures, and acknowledge that there will be obstacles. But you will learn from your mistakes and the mistakes of others, for there is very little learning in success.

Michael Dell
University of Texas at Austin 2003

And I need to tell you that I would much rather fail at something new than succeed at something old.

Ben Cohen
Hampshire College 1990

The problems of failure are problems of discouragement, of hopelessness, of hunger. You want everything to happen and you want it now - and things go wrong.

I decided that I would do my best in future not to write books just for the money. If I did work I was proud of, and I didn't get the money, at least I'd have the work.

Every now and again, I forget that rule, and whenever I do, the Universe kicks me hard and reminds me.

Neil Gaiman
University of the Arts 2012

I've had a lot of success. I've had a lot of failure.

I've looked good. I've looked bad.

I've been praised. And I've been criticized.

But my mistakes have been necessary.

I've dwelled on my failures today because, as graduates of Harvard, your biggest liability is your need to succeed; your need to always find yourself on the sweet side of the bell curve.

Success is a lot like a bright white tuxedo. You feel terrific when you get it, but then you're desperately afraid of getting it dirty, of spoiling it.

Conan O'Brian
Harvard 2000

In commencement addresses like this, people admonish us: "Take risks. Be willing to fail."

But this has always puzzled me. Do you want a surgeon whose motto is: "I like taking risks?"

We do in fact want people to take risks, to strive for difficult goals, even when the possibility of failure looms. Progress cannot happen otherwise.

But how they do it is what seems to matter.

Researchers at the University of Michigan discovered the answers recently . . . They call them a "Failure to Rescue."

More than anything, this is what distinguished the great from the mediocre.

They didn't fail less. They rescued more.

This in fact may be the real story of human and societal improvement. Risk is necessary. Things can, and will, go wrong.

But some have better capacity to prepare for the possibility, to limit the damage, and to sometimes even retrieve success from failure.

Atul Gawande
Williams College 2012

Everybody wants to be a success but no one wants to stop and understand what it takes to succeed.

What it takes to succeed is to understand that *failure is part of the process*. There is no success without failure. There is no success without *multiple* failures. I promise you that.

James Carville
Hobart & William Smith Colleges 2013

Sometimes the desire to be perfect can paralyse us - because we are so afraid of making mistakes. Strive for excellence, but know that achieving excellence involves a lot of falling down along the way.

When Babe Ruth the famous baseball player retired, he had more home runs than any player in history. But he also had more strikeouts than any other player in history.

The point is, you cannot succeed unless you are willing to fail.

Jehane Noujaim
Northwestern University, Qatar May 2014

You will have failures in your life, but it is what you do during those valleys that will determine the heights of your peaks.

Rahm Emanuel
George Washington University 2009

23

Don't be afraid of failure.

Fear of failure is a far worse condition than failure itself, because it kills off possibilities.

Michael Eisner
Denison University 1989

Remember that real success is maximizing your internally derived happiness.

It will not come from external status or money or praise. It will come from a feeling of contribution.

A feeling that you are using your gifts in the best way possible.

Salman Khan
MIT University 2012

It doesn't matter how far you might rise - at some point you are bound to stumble.

Because if you're constantly doing what we do - raising the bar - if you're constantly pushing yourself higher, the law of averages, not to mention the Myth of Icarus, predicts that you will at some point fall.

And when you do I want you to know this, remember this: There is no such thing as failure.

Failure is just life trying to move us in another direction.

Now when you're down there in the hole, it looks like failure.

And when you're down in the hole, when that moment comes, it's really okay to feel bad for a little while.

Give yourself time to mourn what you think you may have lost, but then here's the key: Learn from every mistake.

Because every experience, encounter, and particularly your mistakes are there to teach you and force you into being more who you are.

Oprah Winfrey
Harvard 2013

There is no question in my own mind that failure is the foundation on which the greatest prayers are built - and that one can never fully savour the satisfactions of accomplishment unless one can contrast the feelings of hopes dashed or goals missed, by way of contrast

James B Stewart
De Pauw University 1989

I have the good fortune to be surrounded by some brilliant, intuitive thinkers who create the most elegant and extraordinary products in the world.

For all of us intuition is not a substitute for rigorous thinking and hard work - it is simply the lead-in.

We never take shortcuts. We attend to every detail.

We follow where curiosity leads, aware that the journey may be longer but will ultimately be more worthwhile.

We take risks knowing that risk will sometimes result in failure - but without the possibility of failure, there is no possibility of success.

Tim Cook
Auburn University 2010

Remember that the fear of failure is the most paralysing of all human emotions. Fear of failure stops more people from trying and from doing good, from daring, from succeeding. It truly is to be avoided at all costs - because it kills off possibilities.

Mark Shields
University of Notre Dame 1997

Nobody else is paying as much attention to your failures as you are.

You're the only ones who are obsessed with the importance of your own life. To everyone else, it's just a blip on the radar screen.

So just move on.

Jerry Zucker
University of Wisconsin 2003

Choose the opportunities that are most rewarding, not financially, but personally and professionally. That is how I define passion.

The most successful people I know love what they do. If you choose to do things that you are passionate about, you will not only do them better, but most importantly, you'll be a significantly happier person.

Robert Kraft
Suffolk University 2013

Don't be afraid to shoot the long ball. Take the risk. Life is too short to spend your time avoiding failure . . .

Not every risk will work out, but that's ok. Failure is the world's best teacher.

Michael Bloomberg
University of North Carolina 2012

In order to be successful you have to be brave enough to try . . . and fail.

Katie Couric
Trinity College 2014

The problems of failure are hard.

The problems of success can be harder, because nobody warns you about them.

The first problem of any kind of even limited success is the unshakable conviction that you are getting away with something.

And that any moment now they will discover you. It's Imposter Syndrome

Neil Gaiman
University of the Arts 2012

My idea of success is different today. And as you grow you'll realize the definition of success changes . . .

For me, the most important thing in your life is to live your life with integrity; and not to give into peer pressure to try to be something that you're not . . .

. . . to live your life as an honest and compassionate person; to contribute in some way.

Ellen Degeneres
Tulane University 2009

We all have to decide for ourselves what constitutes failure, but the world is quite eager to give you a set of criteria, if you let it.

J K Rowling
Harvard 2008

31

I wonder why this society in general has such a strange and inaccurate definition of success.

And I think part of it might be because we tend to concentrate on that which we can measure.

The ironic part is that things which are easiest to measure are the least important.

It's the intangibles - caring, spirit, joy, intuition, love, warmth, trust - *those* are the things that matter most,

And those are the things that our society values least - because we can't quantify them.

Ben Cohen
Hampshire College 1990

What's success anyway?

Is success about making the most money? No, money, for the most part, turns people into jerks . . .

So how will we know we've done it right? What's the ultimate measure of success? Then what's the key to success?

In my experience, quite simply, success is happiness.

Chris Sacca
University of Minnesota 2011

It is a myth that the sum of your talents is equal to the sum of your pay check. Talent, like success, is what you define it to be.

Cathleen Black
Simmons College 1990

33

I think it is misleading to talk about success without also referencing failure. I know of no one who has achieved something significant without also in their own lives experiencing their share of hardship, frustration, and regret.

So don't believe that something in your past prevents you from doing great work in the future.

Tim Cook
Auburn University 2010

There are times when you are going to do well, and times when you're going to fail. But neither the doing well, nor the failure, is the measure of success.

The measure of success is what you think about what you've done

Marc S Lewis
University of Texas at Austin 2000

34

Each day that you are working on the journey towards achieving your dreams, while being true to yourself, *that* is success. Write the story of your life that you want to tell when you are old and gray.

Jehane Noujaim
Northwestern University, Qatar, 2014

The problem with all of us sometimes is we convince ourselves of all the reasons we *can't* do something before we even try.

We think *small*, so that we might succeed at that *small* dream we set out for ourselves, in order to avoid failure.

Think of what you might accomplish if you directed all that compelling, forceful energy toward convincing yourself why you CAN do it.

Savannah Guthrie
Hobart & William Smith Colleges 2012

You will be wounded many times in your life. You'll make mistakes. Some people will call them failures, but I have learned that failure is really God's way of saying: "Excuse me, you're moving in the wrong direction."

It's just an experience. Just an experience

Oprah Winfrey
Wellesley College 1997

You might never fail on the scale I did, but some failure in life is inevitable.

It is impossible to live without failing at something - unless you live so cautiously that you might as well not have lived at all.

In which case, you fail by default.

J K Rowling
Harvard 2008

Famous 'Failures'

Because, even those who are famous and successful today once 'failed' – some more than once!

I'm just happy that the Crimson has called me "Harvard's most successful dropout".

I guess that makes me valedictorian of my own special class . . .

I did the best of everyone who failed.

Bill Gates
Harvard 2007

Famous 'Failures'

Reggie Jackson struck out twenty-six hundred times in his career, the most in the history of baseball.

But you don't hear about the strikeouts. People remember the home runs.

Fall forward.

Thomas Edison conducted 1,000 failed experiments. Did you know that? I didn't know that because the 1,001st was the light bulb.

Fall forward.

Every failed experiment is one step closer to success.

Denzel Washington
University of Pennsylvania 2011

Famous 'Failures'

When I graduated from college, I went abroad to study philosophy. I hoped to become a philosopher, but I proved to be profoundly mediocre in the field.

I tried starting a rock band. You don't want to know how awful the songs I wrote were. I wrote one song, for example, comparing my love for a girl to the decline of Marxism.

After this, I worked in government on health care legislation.

That not only went nowhere, it set back the prospect of health reform almost two decades.

But the only failure is the failure to rescue something.

Famous 'Failures'

I took away ideas and experiences, and relationships with people that profoundly changed what I was able to do when I finally found the place that was for me - which was in medicine.

Atul Gawande
Williams College 2012

Famous 'Failures'

So I think it fair to say that by any conventional measure, a mere seven years after my graduation day, I had failed on an epic scale.

An exceptionally short-lived marriage had imploded, and I was jobless, a lone parent, and as poor as it is possible to be in modern Britain, without being homeless.

The fears that my parents had had for me, and that I had had for myself, had both come to pass - and by every usual standard, I was the biggest failure I knew.

J K Rowling
Harvard 2008

41

Surviving Challenges

In 2000, I told graduates to not be afraid to fail, and I still believe that.

But today I tell you that, whether you fear it or not, disappointment will come.

The beauty is that through disappointment you can gain clarity, and with clarity comes conviction and true originality.

Conan O'Brien
Dartmouth College 2011

Life is not easy for anyone. Sometimes you don't see the challenges on the outside, but every single one of us has both those, and everything that goes on inside as well.

Give it your all. Dare to be all you can be.

Hillary Rodham Clinton
SUNY Buffalo 2006

Surviving Challenges

View stressful, political interactions as nothing more than a deeply immersive strategy game.

One that can be won if you stay focused on what matters most, and your emotions and ego are not tied to your argument.

Salman Khan
MIT University 2012

Life is filled with circuses. You will fail. You will likely fail often.

It will be painful. It will be discouraging. At times it will test you to your very core.

But if you want to change the world, don't be afraid of the circuses.

William McRaven
University of Texas 2014

As you travel through life, in these many years ahead, I guarantee that . . .

You will experience loss, heartache, the death of a loved one. You'll probably have to say goodbye to a lover. You'll experience rejection, maybe even have to deal with a bad diagnosis. You'll age.

The trick isn't to avoid these times or pretend they're not happening. You can't.

What you'll need to do is step up to them courageously and embrace them.

Allow these experiences to permeate your being and weave them all into the fabric of your life.

They will not only soften you and strengthen you, you will open your heart to compassion.

You will not be powerless in this either. If you embrace what is happening, instead of denying.

If life gives you lemons, grab it by the horns and drive.

Jane Lynch
Smith College 2012

If you run out of hope at the end of the day, to rise in the morning and put it on again with your shoes - hope is the only reason you won't give in, burn what's left of the ship and go down with it . . .

You have to love that so earnestly - you, who were born into the Age of Irony. Imagine getting caught with your optimism hanging out. It feels so risky.

Barbara Kingsolver
Duke University 2008

I asked women to tell me what their wildest dreams were. Our intention was to fulfil their wildest dreams. We got 77,000 letters.

To our disappointment we found that the deeper the wound, the smaller the dreams. So many women had such small visions, such small dreams for their lives, that we had a difficult time coming up with dreams to fulfil.

Turn your wounds into wisdom.

Oprah Winfrey
Wellesley College 1997

That choice, between the devil and the dream, comes up every day in different little disguises. My advice is to look the dilemma in the face and decide what you can live with.

Meryl Streep
Vassar College 1983

Surviving Challenges

Whenever your life seems hardest . . . there is the chance to find deeper and greater powers within yourself.

Well, you go on. Your journey continues.

You will have encounters with monsters and demons who symbolize your limitations. As each of these is conquered, your consciousness is enlarged and your possibilities expand.

This is your life.
This is your journey.

You are the Hero.

Lee Smith
Hollins College 1993

There will be times when the crisis is going to feel overwhelming. But whenever it starts to get you down, just remember one thing.

Remember that the Chinese word for "crisis" is composed of two picture characters: One for the word "danger" and one for the word "opportunity".

Norman B Rice
Whitman College 1998

Everything in your life is happening to teach you more about yourself. So, even in a crisis, be grateful.

When disappointed, be grateful. When things aren't going the way you want them to, be grateful that you have sense enough to turn it around.

Oprah Winfrey
Howard University 2007

To live life at its fullest you have to have the chutzpah to accept challenges.

You don't need nerves of steel. I'm not saying that sometimes you won't be shaking in your boots after accepting some major challenge. But you can't let that stop you.

'Dr Ruth' Westheimer
Trinity College 2004

Never give in.
Never give in.

Never, never, never, never - in nothing, great or small, large or petty - never give in, except to convictions of honour and good sense.

Winston Churchill
Harrow School 1941

The very least you can do in your life is to figure out what you hope for.

The most you can do is live inside that hope, running down its hallways, touching the walls on both sides.

Barbara Kingsolver
Duke University 2008

You will never truly know yourself, or the strength ot your relationships, until both have been tested by adversity.

Such knowledge is a true gift, for all that it is painfully won, and it has been worth more than any qualification I ever earned.

J K Rowling
Harvard 2008

Being Human(e)

In the course of your lives, without any plan on your part, you'll come to see suffering that will break your heart.

When it happens, and it will, don't turn away from it. Turn toward it. That is the moment when change is born.

Bill & Melinda Gates
Stanford 2014

Do all the other things, the ambitious things - travel, get rich, get famous, innovate, lead, fall in love, make and lose fortunes, swim naked in wild jungle rivers (after first having it tested for monkey poop).

But as you do, to the extent that you can, err in the direction of kindness.

George Saunders
Syracuse University 2013

Real progress requires an authentic way of being, honesty, and above all empathy.

The single most important lesson I learned in 25 years, talking every single day to people, was that there is a common denominator in our human experience.

The common denominator that I found in every single interview is we want to be validated.

We want to be understood.

Make sure that the speed and distance and anonymity of our world doesn't cause us to lose our ability to stand in somebody else's shoes and recognize all that we share as a people.

Oprah Winfrey
Harvard 2013

When you see someone who does something great, tell them about it.

Tell their bosses about it. Tell their family about it . . .

People recognize that you are a source of positivity, and when you're source of positivity people will just naturally gravitate to you.

Salman Khan
Rice University 2012

Respect people with less power then you.

I don't care if you're the most powerful cat in the room, I will judge you on how you treat the least powerful.

Tim Minchin
University of Western Australia 2013

Being Human(e)

You are entering a different business world than I entered.

Mine was just starting to get connected. Yours is hyper-connected.

Mine was competitive. Yours is way more competitive.

Mine moved quickly. Yours moves even more quickly.

As traditional structures are breaking down, leadership has to evolve as well. You'll have to rely on what you know.

Your strength will not come from your place on some org chart - your strength will come from building trust and earning respect.

You're going to need talent, skill, and imagination and vision.

But more than anything else, you're going to need the ability to communicate authentically: To speak so that you inspire the people around you. And to listen. So that you continue to learn each and every day on the job.

Sheryl Sandberg
Harvard Business School 2012

The people who say technology has disconnected you from others are wrong. So are the people who say technology automatically connects you to others. Technology is just a tool. It's a powerful tool, but it's just a tool.

Deep human connection is very different. It's not a tool. It's not a means to an end. It *is* the end

Melinda Gates
Duke University 2013

My best advice to you is, no matter what your profession is, don't be a jerk. It just doesn't pay to be a jerk.

When you talk about climbing the ladder of success it really pays to be kind to the ones you need along the way.

Kindness, respect and all that good stuff - it just goes a long way.

Sutton Foster
Ball State University 2012

Don't ever forget that you're a citizen of this world and there are things you can do to lift the human spirit. Things that are easy; things that are free; things that you can do every day: Civility, respect, kindness, character.

Aaron Sorkin
Syracuse University 2012

Being Human(e)

The people who consider themselves very happy are not in the very poorest nations, as you might guess, nor in the very richest.

The winners are Mexico, Ireland, Puerto Rico - the kinds of places we identify with extended family, noisy villages, a lot of dancing.

The happiest people are the ones with the most community. This could be your key to a new order. You don't need so much stuff to fill your life, when you have people in it.

Barbara Kingsolver
Duke University 2008

Social networking is no substitute for being social. A virtual life is no substitute for really living.

Katie Couric
Boston University 2011

Make people feel that you care about them. And here's, a well, a little secret, the best way to do this is to actually care about them.

Make people feel that you are listening to them. Another little secret, the best way to do this is to actually listen.

Salman Khan
MIT University 2012

Always remember that the moments we have with friends and family, the chances we have to do things that might make a big difference in the world - or even to make a small difference to the ones we love. All those wonderful chances that life gives us - life also takes away.

It can happen fast, and a whole lot sooner than you think.

Larry Page
University of Michigan 2009

What I regret most in my life are failures of kindness.

Those moments when another human being was there, in front of me, suffering, and I responded . . . sensibly. Reservedly. Mildly.

Or, to look at it from the other end of the telescope: Who, in your life, do you remember most fondly, with the most undeniable feelings of warmth?

Those who were kindest to you, I bet.

It's a little facile, maybe, and certainly hard to implement, but I'd say, as a goal in life, you could do worse than:

Try to be kinder.

George Saunders
Syracuse University 2013

Understanding that you can't truly take credit for your successes, nor truly blame others for their failures, will humble you and make you more compassionate.

Tim Minchin

University of Western Australia 2013

Don't cover for your inexperience . . . You have to be confident in your potential *and* aware of your inexperience. And that's really tough.

There are moments when you'll have a different point of view because you're a fresh set of eyes; because you don't care how it's been done before; because you're sharp and creative; because there is another way, a better way.

Jon Lovett

Pitzer 2013

You should live for the future and the things that you really care about. And what are those things?

To figure this out, you need to actually turn off your computer. I know this is difficult. You need to turn off your phone.

You need to actually look at the people who are near you and around you, and decide that it is humans who ultimately are the most important thing to us - not the other aspects.

Eric Schmidt
Carnegie-Mellon University 2009

Try helping others to reach their potential.

Like magic, it will come back ten-fold and help you find your own.

Denise Di Novi
Simmons College 1997

Staying True To You

It might not seem like it sometimes, but you are 100 per cent unique. You are you and no one else is. That's your potential value.

You just need to figure out how to apply it.

Anders Holm
University of Wisconsin-Madison 2013

Your time is limited - so don't waste it living someone else's life.

Don't be trapped by dogma - which is living with the results of other people's thinking.

Don't let the noise of others' opinions drown out your own inner voice.

Steve Jobs
Stanford 2005

65

As we track the unfolding disruption of natural and global stabilities, you will be told to buy into business as usual: You need a job: Trade your future for an entry level position . . .

In the awful moment when someone demands at gunpoint: "Your money or your life" . . .

That's not supposed to be a hard question.

Barbara Kingsolver
Duke University 2008

I guess if I want to say anything it's "Be you." Be true to you - and that should make the ride a little more interesting.

Whoopi Goldberg
SCAD Savannah 2011

If I learned one thing, it is that self-doubt is one of the most destructive forces. It makes you defensive instead of open; reactive instead of active.

Self-doubt is consuming and cruel - and my hope today is that we can all collectively agree to ban it.

Please know, from here on out, you are enough . . . and dare I say, more than enough.

Jennifer Lee
University of New Hampshire 2014

And it's not parroting your parents, or even the thoughts of your learned teachers. It is, now more than ever, about understanding yourself - so you can *become* yourself.

Joss Whedon
Wesleyan University 2013

STAYING TRUE TO YOU

Do the stuff that only you can do.

The urge, starting out, is to copy. And that's not a bad thing. Most of us only find our own voices after we've sounded like a lot of other people.

But the one thing that you have that nobody else has - is you.

So write and draw and build and play and dance - and live as only you can.

Neil Gaiman
University of the Arts 2012

The way to be happy is to like yourself.

And the way to like yourself is to do only things that make you proud.

Marc S Lewis
University of Texas at Austin 2000

I don't believe we have a professional self from Mondays through Fridays, and a real self for the rest of the time.

That kind of division probably never worked, but in today's world - with a real voice, an authentic voice - it makes even less sense.

I talk about my hopes and fears and ask people about theirs.

I try to be myself.

Honest about my strengths and weaknesses - and I encourage others to do the same.

It is all professional and it is all personal - all at the very same time.

Sheryl Sandberg
Harvard Business School 2012

If living is the trick, what's crucial for you is to do something that makes the best use of your own gifts, and your own individuality.

There's only one you. Don't ever let anyone persuade you that you're somebody else.

William Zinsser
Wesleyan University 1988

Don't waste your time trying to succeed at other people's dreams, or dreams you don't believe in.

Only your real dreams will satisfy you. Those are the dreams that will give you the best chance of leaving your mark on the world.

Those are the dreams that are worth failing for, and taking the big risks for.

Jehane Noujaim
Northwestern University 2014

We spend too much of our lives trying to live up to the expectations of others.

We buy things we don't really want with money we don't really have to impress people we don't really care about.

Forget that; forget what other people think.

Chris Sacca
University of Minnesota 2011

But don't limit yourselves.

The most gregarious among us are far more insecure than we would ever admit. We all go through life bristling at our external limitations . . . but the most difficult chains to break are inside us.

Bradley Whitford
University of Wisconsin 2004

Please, I beg of you, never forget this – FUN! Don't ever abandon that intoxicating sense of fun in your art.

Through that, you are serving your truth. My hope for you is that you will let that truth guide you in every moment of your journey. If you can find that, you have everything.

That's why "making it" is, in the end, utterly insignificant. *Living* it, *breathing* it, *serving* it . . . that's where your joy will lie.

Joyce DiDonato
Juilliard 2014

If you believe in what you're saying; if you believe in what you're doing; you'll be more effective, more passionate and more authentic in everything you do.

Seth Goldman
American University 2010

I called up my father. I told him I was going to quit this job that now promised me millions of dollars, to write a book for an advance of 40 grand.

There was a long pause on the other end of the line . . .

"Stay at Salomon Brothers 10 years, make your fortune, and *then* write your books," he said.

I didn't need to think about it.

I knew what intellectual passion felt like - because I'd felt it here, at Princeton - and I wanted to feel it again.

I was 26 years old. Had I waited until I was 36, I would never have done it. I would have forgotten the feeling.

Michael Lewis
Princeton University 2012

73

To get what you want out of life all you can really do is find out who you are - and do that.

Anders Holm
University of Wisconsin-Madison 2013

When you accept that who you are is enough; you become the biggest participant in making your work and even your relationships better.

Jennifer Lee
University of New Hampshire 2013

My fervent hope for each of you is that somehow your boundless potential will merge with your own internal promise to stay true to yourself, write your own personal narrative, and strive for your unique definition of success.

Katie Couric
Williams College 2007

Survival tip number one for going into the real world is to bring a map with you. A map, by the way, of yourself.

Don't listen to others for directions about who you are.

Diane Sawyer
University of Illinois at Champaign-Urbana 1997

And remember, when you hear yourself saying one day that you don't have time anymore to read, or listen to music, or look at a painting . . .

Then you're getting old.

That means they got you after all.

Susan Sontag
Wellesley College 1983

Know that being honest, both about what you do know and what you don't, can and will pay off . . .

. . . go forward with confidence and an eagerness to learn and to be honest with yourselves, and others, to reject a culture of insincerity by virtue of the example you set in your own lives.

Jon Lovett
Pitzer 2013

If it doesn't feel right, don't do it.

That's the lesson. And that lesson alone will save you, my friends, a lot of grief. If it feels right, move forward. If it doesn't feel right, don't do it.

Oprah Winfrey
Stanford 2008

76

I'm here to tell you there is no price on sleeping well at night.

Worrying to cover-up lies is the loneliest cancer in the world. This is lonely because you can never tell anyone about it, even as it's metastasizing and eating you up inside.

Chris Sacca
University of Minnesota 2011

You should do what you were put here to do. That is the most certain key to success and happiness.

Gabrielle Giffords
Scripps College 2009

My advice to you is to be true to yourself, and everything will be fine.

Ellen Degeneres
Tulane University 2009

77

Staying True To You

You're going to have naysayers, and I'll tell you, you will throughout your life have people who will tell you are not good enough.

Maybe they're jealous. Maybe they think you aren't. Maybe they've had a bad day.

But ultimately you have to believe in yourself.

Meredith Vieira
Tufts University 2008

Stand up for what you believe in.

Take a stand, no matter how unpopular that stand may be.

The world does not honour fence-sitters.

Bill Richardson
Colorado College 1999

78

You must believe in yourself and in your work. Don't believe them when they tell you how bad you are, and how terrible your ideas are.

But also, don't believe them when they start telling you how wonderful you are and how great your ideas are.

Just believe in yourself and believe in your work, and you'll do just fine.

Michael Uslan
Indiana University 2006

Find your own voice.

Like Elizabeth Blackwell, refuse to give into the tyranny of conformity.

Bill Whitaker
Hobart & William Smith Colleges 2008

Find out who you are, what you think. Listen to the sounds of your own heart and everything will be fine.

Goldie Hawn
American University 2002

Networking, resumes, mentors - all these things are important. But work should be an extension of who you are. Anything that leads you to that discovery is golden and its own reward.

Denise Di Novi
Simmons College 1997

Remember, you should never want something so badly that you do something you don't believe in to get it.

Susan Rice
Stanford 2010

You've got little enough time; you don't realize until you're running out of it how little time you have. So I would say to you, in the time you have left, "Make the most of it by making the most of yourself."

Which is doing what means the most to *you*, and not to somebody else.

Malcolm Forbes
Syracuse University 1988

What are those moments when your soul, the essence of who you are, gets expressed into the world? That is what it means to be unleashed.

So don't change yourself. Come home to yourself. Face your tigers. Notice what you're bringing. Shift from automatic to authentic living.

John Jacob Scherer
Roanoke College 2010

Trust, Intuition, And Being Present

Trust, Intuition & Being Present

Your *heart, intuition and dreams* are your ultimate guide.

Follow your heart, your intuition, and your dreams - not other people's dreams or expectations.

The little decisions you make with your head, the big ones you make with your heart and your intuition.

The psychiatrist, Sigmund Freud wrote: "When making a decision of minor importance, I have always found it advantageous to consider all the pros and cons.

In vital matters, however, such as the choice of a mate or a profession, the decision should come from the unconscious, from somewhere within ourselves."

Jehane Noujaim
Northwestern University, Qatar 2014

There is going to come a time in your life when in order to succeed you will have to trust - when you will have to make a big leap of faith.

And when that time comes I hope you will swallow your fear, and get into the wheelbarrow.

Marc S Lewis
University of Texas at Austin 2000

In all things in life, choose your conscience, and trust your instincts, and lead your lives without regrets.

It's simply easier that way.

David Halberstam
Dartmouth College 1996

84

As you get ready to walk out under the bright lights of the improvisational stage of the rest of your life, I implore you to learn those two lessons I learned years ago.

Be bold.

Make courageous choices for yourself.

And secondly; don't always worry about what your next line is supposed to be; what you're supposed to do next. There's no script.

Live your life.

Be in this moment.
Be in this moment.
Now be in *this* moment.

Dick Costolo
University of Michigan 2013

And what I've found is that difficulties come when you don't pay attention to life's whisper - because life always whispers to you first.

And if you ignore the whisper, sooner or later you'll get a scream.

Oprah Winfrey
Stanford 2008

Learn to trust yourself.
That's very vital . . .
Just stand with yourself.

Remember, in his lifetime, Van Gogh sold only two paintings.

I personally sold even fewer.

Eric Idle
Whitman College 2013

In turning important decisions over to intuition one has to give up on the idea of developing a life plan that will bear any resemblance to what ultimately unfolds.

Intuition is something that occurs in the moment, and if you are open to it - If you listen to it - it has the potential to direct or redirect you in a way that is best for you.

Tim Cook
Auburn University 2010

Listen to the whispers inside you.

We have a lot of problems in this world and we're going to need you to think outside the box.

Bradley Whitford
University of Wisconsin 2004

In baseball, high-percentage hitters know better: it's "focus" they talk about.

Psychologists describe skilled rock climbers, and tennis players, and pianists as going beyond focus, to what they have called a "flow" experience - a sense of absorption with the rock or the ball or the music, in which the "me versus it" disappears and there's a kind of oneness with the task that brings a joyful higher awareness, as well as successful performance.

I've had these experiences, too little but not too late, and probably you have, too.

They are a supreme kind of pleasure.

You will have more of them if you do one thing at a time.

John Walsh
Wheaton College 2000

When I graduated from college, I spent a lot of time thinking about how cool it would be to be on the Johnny Carson show.

A few years later, it happened. We were dreadful.

Eventually I got over the embarrassment, but I never got those years back - years I spent waiting for some future event to make me happy.

I had tricked myself into thinking, "As soon as I get there, I'll be OK."

Jerry Zucker
University of Wisconsin-Madison 2003

And the key to life is to develop an internal moral, emotional G.P.S. that can tell you which way to go.

Oprah Winfrey
Harvard 2013

What is the thing that gives you so much joy you'd do it for free? And what if you don't know what that thing is yet . . .

Do something else for a while - but keep listening for that inner voice. Take some time everyday to separate yourself from the world so that it can be heard. It will call you if you're listening.

Denise Di Novi
Simmons College 1997

You have to leave the city of your comfort and go into the wilderness of your intuition.

You can't get there by bus, only by hard work and risk, and by not quite knowing what you're doing. But what you'll discover will be wonderful. What you'll discover will be yourself.

Alan Alda
Connecticut College 1980

Recognize the power of presence. Do not allow yourself to be distracted. Know your life purpose, and the contribution you want to make to society.

Deepak Chopra
Hartwick College 2013

You can't connect the dots looking forward; you can only connect them looking backwards. So you have to trust that the dots will somehow connect in your future.

You have to trust in something - your gut, destiny, life, karma, whatever.

This approach has never let me down, and it has made all the difference in my life.

Steve Jobs
Stanford 2005

The Road
Less Travelled

My counsel to you: Let life surprise you. Don't have a plan. Plans are for wusses.

If my life went according to my plan, I would never ever have the life I have today. . .

Don't deprive yourself of the exciting journey your life can be when you relinquish the need to have goals and a blueprint.

Jane Lynch
Smith College 2012

Go, and make interesting mistakes. Make amazing mistakes. Make glorious and fantastic mistakes.

Break rules. Leave the world more interesting for your being here.

Neil Gaiman
University of the Arts 2012

Make career decisions the same way you fill out your tournament brackets. Follow your heart, and go with your gut.

Do what you love, find a way to get paid for it and, if you ever have the luxury of multiple job offers, don't make the decision based on salary alone.

Michael Bloomberg
University of North Carolina 2012

You may feel that one voice, when a thousand are needed to make things change, is not enough.

But you are wrong. One articulate voice can attract a thousand more. It is important for one of you out there to be that voice.

Beverly Sills
Dartmouth College 1985

94

Personal happiness lies in knowing that life is not a checklist of acquisition or achievement. Your qualifications, your CV, are not your life. Though you will meet many people of my age, and older, who confuse the two.

J K Rowling
Harvard 2008

I've found that nothing in life is worthwhile unless you take risks. Nothing.

Denzel Washington
University of Pennsylvania 2011

Try not to get a regular job. When you have a regular job, you wind up acting like regular people.

Jay Leno
Emerson College 2014

95

I didn't understand it then, as a young MBA student, but life has a habit of throwing you curve balls.

Don't get me wrong, it's good to plan for the future.

But - if you're like me, and you occasionally want to swing for the fences - you can't count on a predictable life.

Tim Cook
Auburn University 2010

In your rainbow journey toward the realization of personal goals, don't make choices based on your security and your safety.

Nothing is safe.

Toni Morrison
Barnard College 1979

I urge you to do whatever you do for no reason other than you love it, and believe in its importance.

Don't bother with work you don't believe in any more than you would a spouse you're not crazy about . . .

Resist the easy comforts of complacency, the specious glitter of materialism, the narcotic paralysis of self-satisfaction.

David McCullough Jr
Wellesley High School 2012

My suggestion is to "go forth" and "boldly stride" - yes - but to make sure, and this is important, to have some fun.

Enjoy it. Lighten up. Laugh a little.

Chris Regan
Ithaca 2014

97

Take your time, do not be in a hurry. And do not think you need to achieve everything right here, right now.

Savannah Guthrie
Hobart & William Smith Colleges 2012

There is nothing more rewarding than embracing a cause that is bigger than yourself.

Katie Couric
Trinity College 2014

I know it seems like the world is crumbling out there, but it is actually a great time in your life to get a little crazy.

Follow your curiosity, and be ambitious about it. Don't give up on your dream.

Larry Page
University of Michigan 2009

There is no such thing as not worshipping. Everybody worships.

The only choice we get is *what* to worship.

And an outstanding reason for choosing some sort of God, or spiritual-type thing to worship . . . is that pretty much anything else you worship will eat you alive.

If you worship money and things - if they are where you tap real meaning in life - then you will never have enough. Never feel you have enough. It's the truth.

Worship your own body and beauty, and sexual allure and you will always feel ugly. And when time and age start showing, you will die a million deaths before they finally plant you.

Worship power - you will feel weak and afraid, and you will need ever more power over others to keep the fear at bay.

THE ROAD LESS TRAVELLED

Worship your intellect, being seen as smart - you will end up feeling stupid, a fraud, always on the verge of being found out.

And so on . . .

Look, the insidious thing about these forms of worship is not that they're evil or sinful.

It is that they are unconscious. They are default-settings.

They're the kind of worship you just gradually slip into, day after day - getting more and more selective about what you see, and how you measure value, without ever being fully aware that that's what you're doing.

David Foster Wallace
Kenyon College 2005

100

From here on out you have to switch gears.

You're no longer meeting and exceeding expectations. There are no expectations. There's no script.

Dick Costolo
University of Michigan 2013

A couple of hundred years ago . . . the Iroquois Federation of tribes, in the North Eastern part of North America, was a governing body that made all important decisions on the basis of one rule - and that was the seven generations question.

That is, they would ask: "How does this decision, how does this act that we are about to undertake today, affect the world seven generations from now?"

Barbara Kingsolver
DePauw University 1994

101

The closed circle of pure materialism is clear to us now.

Aspirations become wants, wants become needs, and self-gratification becomes a bottomless pit.

Mario Cuomo
Iona College 1984

I hope you find true meaning, contentment and passion in your life.

I hope that you navigate the hard times and you come out with greater strength and resolve.

I hope that whatever balance you seek, you find it with your eyes wide open.

Sheryl Sandberg
Barnard College 2011

102

Believe that the sort of life you wish to live is, at this very moment, just waiting for you to summon it up.

And when you wish for it, you begin moving toward it.

And it, in turn, begins moving toward you.

Suzan-Lori Parks
Mount Holyoke 2001

It's important to acknowledge the value and power of unorthodoxy.

Annie Lennox
Berklee College of Music 2013

Make bigger choices.
Take courageous risks.

Dick Costolo
University of Michigan 2013

103

Don't bother to have a plan at all.

All that stuff about plan, throw that out.

It seems to me that it's all about opportunity, and make your own luck.

Eric Schmidt
Carnegie-Mellon University 2009

Here's a goal for real life, worth setting and then striving for daily:

To be thankful, whatever your circumstances, every step of the way.

Savannah Guthrie
Hobart & William Smith Colleges 2012

If I have learned anything in my time traveling the world, it is the power of hope.

The power of one person - Washington, Lincoln, King, Mandela and even a young girl from Pakistan - Malala.

One person can change the world by giving people hope.

William McRaven
University of Texas 2014

I have looked in the mirror every morning and asked myself: "If today were the last day of my life, would I want to do what I am about to do today?"

And whenever the answer has been "No" for too many days in a row, I know I need to change something.

Steve Jobs
Stanford 2005

Most of the academic world operates as if we believe that the critical skill society needs of us is to know the right answers.

Too often, as a result, we overlook an obvious fact: finding the right answer is impossible unless we have asked the right question . . .

The valuable skill, I realized, was to ask the right question.   That done, getting the right answer was typically quite straightforward.

Clayton Christensen
South New Hampshire University 2009

My advice to you is be afraid of old ideas - not new ideas

Duncan Niederauer
Colgate University 2013

106

Never turn down a job because of the money. Only turn it down because you don't like it. Money will come later. Don't even worry about it.

Jay Leno
Emerson College 2014

We're in a transitional world right now . . . Which is, on the one hand, intimidating, and on the other, immensely liberating.

The rules, the assumptions, the now-we're-supposed-to's of how you get your work seen, and what you do then, are breaking down. The gatekeepers are leaving their gates . . .

The old rules are crumbling and nobody knows what the new rules are. So make up your own rules.

Neil Gaiman
University of the Arts 2012

107

Don't be afraid to be a fool.

Remember, you cannot be both young and wise. Young people who pretend to be wise to the ways of the world are mostly just cynics.

Cynicism masquerades as wisdom, but it is the farthest thing from it. Because cynics don't learn anything. Because cynicism is a self-imposed blindness; a rejection of the world because we are afraid it will hurt us or disappoint us. Cynics always say no.

But saying "Yes" begins things.

Saying "Yes" is how things grow. Saying "Yes" leads to knowledge. "Yes" is for young people.

So for as long as you have the strength to, say "Yes!"

Stephen Colbert
Knox College 2006

Baseball players say they don't have to look to see if they hit a home run - they can feel it.

So I wish for you a moment, a moment soon, when you really put the bat on the ball, when you really get a hold of one and drive it into the upper deck.

When you *feel* it.

When you aim high and hit your target.

When, just for a moment, all else disappears and you soar with wings as eagles.

Aaron Sorkin

Syracuse University 2012

A Life of

Heart & Passion

Use your time to do what you love. Don't waste a moment doubting your heart, or fearing a risk.

Believe that anything in life is possible and, with determination and passion, make that belief come true . . .

Remember, you are the author of your own life; it is up to you how you write it. With courage, integrity, kindness and great friends you will find your true path.

Jehane Noujaim
Northwestern University, Qatar 2014

I stopped trying to make my life perfect, and instead tried to make it interesting. I wanted my story to be an adventure - and that's made all the difference.

Drew Houston
Massachusetts Institute of Technology 2013

Fall in love with the process and the results will follow.

You've got to want to do whatever you want to do more than you want to be whatever you want to be.

Life is too challenging for external rewards to sustain us.

The joy is in the journey.

Bradley Whitford
University of Wisconsin 2004

A quote from Howard Thurman:
"Don't ask yourself what the world needs. Ask yourself what makes you come alive, and then go do that. Because what the world needs is people who have come alive."

Oprah Winfrey
Harvard 2013

112

This prevailing notion that you have to choose between your ideals and your professional life . . .

It's a myth that it takes compromising your hopes and dreams, ambitions and beliefs.

No matter what path we choose in life, each of us can find a way to answer that calling that I believe is within each of us - to find a way to make a difference in the world.

Dan Glickman
Hobart & William Smith Colleges 2010

Continue to share your heart with people even if its been broken. Don't treat your heart like an action figure wrapped in plastic and never used.

Amy Poehler
Harvard 2011

113

You will need to find your passion . . .

Many of you may take until your 30's or 40's but don't give up on finding it because then all you're doing is waiting on the Reaper.

Find your passion and follow it.

Randy Pausch
Carnegie-Mellon University 2008

So many of us choose our path out of fear disguised as practicality . . .

You can fail at what you don't want. So you might as well take a chance on doing what you love.

Jim Carrey
Maharishi University of Management 2014

Pursuing something you love should be the first thing on your post-graduate to do list. But too often, that's not what drives young people as they look at their life goals.

According to a recent survey, many say their top two priorities are: Number 1, being rich, and Number 2, being famous. Believe me, it's not all it's cracked up to be.

Remember, Bill Gates started Microsoft loving computers, not loving money.

Katie Couric
Williams College 2007

If you can . . . fall in love - with the work, with people you work with, with your dreams and their dreams.

Robert Krulwich
Berkeley Journalism School 2011

Some of the most miserable people I have ever met have been people who chose their careers based on its level of salary or prestige.

They focused on the externalities, at the expense of what truly made them happy inside.

This is exactly the wrong way to make a life for yourself.

It leaves you empty and thirsty at the end of it, and does no good for those who are close to you and those in your community.

Material things never satisfy. Find what it is that you love and pursue it with courage and confidence.

Gabrielle Giffords
Scripps College 2009

Pursue whatever it is that you want to do with your life.

It is the only secret to happiness that I know. Except for maybe true love.

Lewis Black
University of California at San Diego 2013

Forget about the fast lane.

If you really want to fly, just harness your power to your passion.

Honor your calling. Everybody has one.

Trust your heart, and success will come to you.

Oprah Winfrey
Stanford 2008

117

In my experience, you will truly serve only what you love because, as the prophet says, service is love made visible.

If you love friends, you will serve your friends.

If you love community, you will serve your community.

If you love money, you will serve your money.

And if you love only yourself, you will serve only yourself. And you will have only yourself.

So, no more winning. Instead, try to love others and serve others, and hopefully, find those who love and serve you in return.

Stephen Colbert
Northwestern University 2011

If you think it's a rat race - before you drop out, take a deep breath.

Maybe you picked the wrong job. Try again. And then try again.

Try until you find something that stirs your passion, a job that matters to you and matters to others.

It is the ultimate luxury to combine passion and contribution. It's also a very clear path to happiness

Sheryl Sandberg
Barnard College 2011

So focus on what stirs your soul – because it's hard to excel at anything that you don't love.

Susan Rice
Stanford 2010

119

I don't know that it's an issue for anybody but me, but it's true that nothing I did, where the only reason for doing it was the money, was ever worth it. Except as bitter experience.

The things I did because I was excited, and wanted to see them exist in reality have never let me down. And I've never regretted the time I spent on any of them.

Neil Gaiman
University of the Arts 2012

Follow your dream - even if it seems risky and the odds seem overwhelming - whatever it may be. You will always regret it if you didn't give if your best shot.

M L Flynn
Hollins College 1995

Find the joy. Life goes by in an instant.

In this fast-paced, crazy world, slow down enough to appreciate and revel in the many things you will experience - a baby's smile, the beautiful symmetry of a cherry blossom, the embrace of a comforted friend, the spectacular palate of a desert sunset.

Katie Couric
Williams College 2007

Don't think about what you want from life. Think about what life wants from you. If you're observant, some large problem will plop itself in front of you. It will define your mission and your calling.

Your passion won't come from inside. It will come from outside.

David Brooks
Sewanee University of the South 2013

A Life of Heart & Passion

When you are deciding what to do, don't do it because it's safe and sensible, or because others expect it.

Though we all need to pay the bills, the biggest mistake you can make is to do something only for the money.

Do something because you love it so much you'll be miserable if you don't.

Denise Di Novi
Simmons College 1997

And keep your friends and family close. They will make your life journey truly rewarding. During the good times, you'll have someone to celebrate with - like today. And during the tough times, you'll have someone to turn to for advice, comfort, and love.

Mary Barra
University of Michigan 2014

Our other tendency - especially when faced with this kind of nakedly adversarial world - is to narrow down, focus on just our own material needs and success.

Why get involved in more when it so often involves dealing with the antagonistic and the unkind?

It's so much simpler and less messy to hold ourselves back and stay removed in our own private realm.

The trouble is, you will wake up one day asking yourself why it is so unfulfilling to simply exist.

You cannot flourish without a larger purpose.

Atul Gawande
University of North Carolina 2014

A LIFE OF HEART & PASSION

My roommate . . . was going to an orientation meeting at the Harvard Lampoon, the school humor magazine, and I decided for some reason to tag along.

I wrote one piece, then I wrote another piece, then another.

Before long, I was running the place,

The only difference was I was joyously happy.

I was succeeding at something because I loved the process, not because I was trying to get anywhere.

I had found the thing I wanted to do for the rest of my life.

Conan O'Brien
Stuyvesant High School 2006

Finding Your
Way Forward

You're all going to be faced with the invitation to create yourselves. And the world will tell you that you need to wait. That you need permission to be the hero you dream yourself to be . . . It's a lie.

You all have goals in your minds . . . Take a second to step back from those goals. Because it's not the goals you want – it's how you think attaining them is going to make you feel about yourself.

But you don't need the goals to feel that way.

Dream yourself to be the hero you see yourself as once those goals are achieved. Be confident. Be sexy. Be important. Don't believe the voice that tells you you need to have something to *be* something.

Brad Falchuk
Hobart & William Smith Colleges 2014

Someone asked me recently how to do something she thought was going to be difficult.

I suggested she pretend that she was someone who could do it.

Not pretend to do it, but pretend she *was* someone who could.

Neil Gaiman
University of the Arts 2012

How do you know what is the right path to choose to get the result that you desire?

The honest answer is this: You won't. And accepting that greatly eases the anxiety of your life experience.

Jon Stewart
The College of William & Mary 2004

127

I'm a big believer in the power of inexperience. It was the greatest asset I had when I started TFA.

If I had known at the outset how hard it was going to be, I might never have started.

Wendy Kopp
Boston University 2013

But the good news is - As long as you aren't stubbornly wrong so frequently that they kick you out of the building, or so meek that everyone forgets you're in the building, you'll learn and grow and get better at striking that balance until your inexperience becomes experience.

So it's a dilemma that solves itself; how awesome is that?

Jon Lovett
Pitzer 2013

In reality, your happiness has a lot more to do with how you see the world, than how the world sees you.

Callie Khouri
Sweet Briar College 1994

I could tell you that when you have trouble making up your mind about something, tell yourself you'll settle it by flipping a coin.

But don't go by how the coin flips. Go by your emotional reaction to the coin flip.

Are you happy or sad it came up heads or tails?

David Brooks
Rice University 2011

129

Every choice lays down a trail of bread crumbs, so that when you look behind you there appears to be a very clear path that points straight to the place where you now stand.

But when you look ahead there isn't a bread crumb in sight. There are just a few shrubs, a bunch of trees, a handful of skittish woodland creatures.

You glance from left to right and find no indication of which way you're supposed to go. And so you stand there, sniffing at the wind, looking for directional clues in the growth patterns of moss, and you think "What now?"

Sometimes not having any idea where we're going works out better than we could possibly have imagined.

Ann Patchett
Sarah Lawrence College 2006

It's better to be a hopeful person than a cynical, grumpy one. Because you have to live in the same world either way, and if you're hopeful, you have more fun . . . and you like yourself better.

Barbara Kingsolver
DePauw University 1994

Free your imaginations so you can become all that you want to be.

Sutton Foster
Ball State University 2012

You have a lifetime of choices. But as you get older you may have fewer choices. Use your power of choice wisely.

Patrick Corvington
Hobart & William Smith Colleges 2011

Never assume that just because it's someone's job, they know how to do it.

And two, don't let yourself be intimidated by professionals, or their uniforms.

Jerry Zucker
University of Wisconsin-Madison 2003

Once you're prepared, throw your preparation in the trash.

The most interesting living in this world has the element of surprise and of genuine, honest discovery.

Be open to that.

Bradley Whitford
University of Wisconsin 2004

The fulfilling life, the distinctive life, the relevant life, is an achievement - not something that will fall into your lap because you're a nice person, or mommy ordered it from the caterer.

You'll note the founding fathers took pains to secure your inalienable right to life, liberty, and the pursuit of happiness.

Quite an active verb, "pursuit" . . .

David McCullough Jr
Wellesley High School 2012

You have an abundance of opportunities before you. But don't spend so much time trying to choose the perfect opportunity, that you miss the *right* opportunity.

Michael Dell
University of Texas at Austin 2003

Persistence. . .

But let me just add:

There is a fine line between persistence and being straight out annoying. Working someone's nerves too much won't get you very far.

I know of countless examples, though, of persistence paying off both in getting the job you want and getting your goals accomplished.

Persistence is critical.

Being creative and persistent is even better.

Katie Couric
Williams College 2007

So to renew the frontier every day, what do you do?

Be uncomfortable.
Open doors.
Empathize with strangers.
Try new things out.
Seek serendipity.
Take chances with new friends.
And pay it forward to people you don't know.

Victor W Hwang
Austin Community College 2014

Don't rush. You don't need to know what you're going to do with the rest of your life.

Most people I know who were sure of their career path at 20 are having mid-life crises now.

Tim Minchin
University of Western Australia 2013

135

When you are 80 years old and in a quiet moment of reflection, narrating for only yourself the most personal version of your life story, the telling that will be most compact and meaningful, will be the series of choices you have made.

In the end, we are our choices.

Build yourself a great story.

Jeff Bezos
Princeton 2010

Life is - this is a John Lennon quote - life is what happens to you while you're busy making other plans.

So live it with its fullness. And if you live your life and forego your plan, you can also forego fear.

Eric Schmidt
Carnegie-Mellon University 2009

Judge yourself not by your accomplishments - but by the happiness of the people around you.

Jerry Zucker
University of Wisconsin-Madison 2003

Dream yourself to be the heroes your teachers, friends and family know you already are.

I think I speak for all of them when I say that I cannot wait to see the dreams your dreams dream to life in the world.

Brad Falchuk
Hobart & William Smith Colleges 2014

How to Deliver a Great Speech

Whether it's Graduation, or any other event, here are some points on producing a speech that people will actually want to listen to

There are some truly great and insightful graduation speeches that have stood the test of time. They still inspire because they pass on nuggets of hard-earned wisdom, while at the same time being interesting and entertaining. They engage their audience.

The great ones fill your heart with warmth and hope, and connect you to their speaker. They resonate. They inspire. They are the rare ones.

And then there are the others. Most speeches are pretty much instantly forgotten. Usually they fade because they are as exciting as tapioca, and bore their listeners into disconnection. For the true horrors, obscurity is just wishful thinking; the worst of them have attained immortality by redefining tedium.

Top Tips for Speakers

Having spent hundreds of hours listening to and reading thousands of speeches – it's been interesting to be able to form an overview.

It quickly becomes obvious what makes a winner. And what does not.

If you're about to write a graduation speech – or any other speech come to think of it – here are some observations.

If you do take the time to read these, your audience will be endlessly grateful.

1 *- It's really not about you. Honestly, really, truly - no-one out there wants to hear your life story. A graduation day is full of excitable kids and their relieved parents. It's their day. They want to know what it is you have to offer them. What can you say that will help them to lead a better life?*

2 - *Be generous. Instead of reinforcing how important and successful you have become, give them something important that life has taught you. Something that will really make them reconsider the status quo, and show them how they can enhance their lives.*

3 - *Share meaningfully. Throughout all your successes, what are the things that are really closest to your heart? What has sustained you? What has the most meaning for you? Why not pass that insight on . . .*

4 - *It's not a biography lesson. (To reinforce #1 above) Presumably if you've been asked to speak you've had a level of success in some arena - however, the very worst and most boring speeches are the backstory: a chronological list of events and accomplishments. They always end up being ego-ridden and dry, dry, dry. If you want them to listen, keep it interesting. Generally what interests people most - is hearing about them, not you.*

5 - *It's not a political rally. If you work in the corridors of power, chances are everyone already knows your stance. Please don't squander this opportunity to add real value to someone's life by reinforcing, or even worse, justifying your own position.*

6 – *Keep it light. You've been invited to talk at a day of celebration. So make your words celebratory. Yes, there may be a lot wrong with the world but this is not the time to dwell on that. Keep focussed on the up-side.*

7 – *Keep it human. The best speakers connect with their audience through the heart. The way to do this is to show them you're human too. Share something that lets them know that.*

8 - *Reframe 'success'. Not all success is quantifiable on the world stage, at the top of the corporate ladder, or within a bank vault. What has your journey through life taught you? Has it changed what 'success' really means to you now?*

Top Tips for Speakers

9 - Don't only talk about success. Not everyone's life will pivot around 'success'. But it's still possible to live a meaningful life. Be inspiring, but not judgmental or confining.

10 – Include Failure. Everyone's life has some. It's the reality of failures and stuff-ups and flaws that make a person interesting, and often more compassionate and nicer to know. Sharing some of yours (even if they're rare) will help you to connect with everyone, and make you much more human and approachable. It will also make you an inspiring example of how you can go on to be a success despite having 'failed' earlier on.

11 – Don't add pressure. There's already enough of that around. Everyone listening to you has the opportunity to 'change the world' but, if that's your focus, frame it as an enticing opportunity. Offer an invitation rather than delivering an obligation. People respond better to enticement than directives.

Top Tips for Speakers

12 – *Create stories. Bring the important points you want to highlight alive. Tell a (brief) story to make them real. And interesting. And memorable.*

13 – *Make 'em laugh. If you can, it always helps. Nothing makes the human heart warm more than laughter. It doesn't have to be stand-up – wryness and wit work well too. Self-deprecation always hits the mark.*

14 – *Make 'em want more. A good speech is a brief speech. Keeping them interested, laughing and there for only a short time will make you well-liked, well-received and well-remembered. The perfect guest speaker in fact!*

Look Who's Talking

Here are some of the people who have been talking to you. Many names you'll recognise instantly, some maybe not. Either way, they're all included in this book not only because of the success they've achieved, but because they have something to offer you.

Also available:

GRADUATION
INSPIRATION

BOOK 2

More Inspiring Quotes from the World's
Most Uplifting Graduation Speeches:
How to Avoid the Hamster Wheel
and Lead the Life You Want

ALISON WILSON

GRADUATION
INSPIRATION

BOOK 3

Yet More Inspiring Quotes from the World's
Most Uplifting Graduation Speeches:
How to Avoid the Hamster Wheel
and Lead the Life You Want

ALISON WILSON

for more details, and many more quotes:
www.graduationinspiration.com